Better Homes and Ga[rdens]

New Junior Garden Book

by Felder Rushing

Meredith® Books
Des Moines, Iowa

Better Homes and Gardens® Books
An imprint of Meredith® Books

New Junior Garden Book
Writer: Felder Rushing
Associate Art Director / Designer: Ken Carlson
Illustration: Wayne Vincent & Associates
Project Photographer: Greg Strelecki
Garden Photographers: Felder Rushing, Sharon Lovejoy
Copy Chief: Catherine Hamrick
Copy and Production Editor: Terri Fredrickson
Contributing Copy Editor: Deborah Gibson, Jay Lamar
Contributing Proofreaders: Neala Ellingson, Debra Morris Smith, Margaret Smith
Indexer: Colleen Johnson
Electronic Production Coordinator: Paula Forest
Editorial and Design Assistants: Kaye Chabot, Treesa Landry, Karen Schirm
Production Director: Douglas M. Johnston
Production Manager: Pam Kvitne
Assistant Prepress Manager: Marjorie J. Schenkelberg

Meredith® Books
Editor in Chief: James D. Blume
Design Director: Matt Strelecki
Managing Editor: Gregory H. Kayko
Executive Garden Editor: Cathy Wilkinson Barash

Director, Sales & Marketing, Retail: Michael A. Peterson
Director, Sales & Marketing, Special Markets: Rita McMullen
Director, Sales & Marketing, Home & Garden Center Channel: Ray Wolf
Director, Operations: George A. Susral

Vice President, General Manager: Jamie L. Martin

***Better Homes and Gardens®* Magazine**
Editor in Chief: Jean LemMon
Executive Garden Editor: Mark Kane

Meredith Publishing Group
President, Publishing Group: Christopher M. Little
Vice President, Consumer Marketing and Development: Hal Oringer

Meredith Corporation
Chairman and Chief Executive Officer: William T. Kerr

Chairman of the Executive Committee: E.T. Meredith III

All of us at Better Homes and Gardens® Books are dedicated to providing you with the information and ideas you need to create great projects. We welcome your comments and suggestions. Write to us at: Better Homes and Gardens® Books, Garden Editorial Department, LN-116, 1716 Locust St., Des Moines, IA 50309–3023.

If you would like to purchase additional copies of any of our books, check wherever books are sold.

First Edition. Printing Number and Year:
5 4 3 2 1 03 02 01 00 99
Library of Congress Catalog Card Number: 98-68021
ISBN: 0-696-20849-0

About the Author:

Felder Rushing lives and gardens with his two children, Ira and Zoe, in Jackson, Mississippi. Many of the projects in this book grace their home and yard.

Felder is a nationally known speaker on a variety of garden topics, and specializes in children's gardening and yard art. He is a national Director of the Garden Writers Association of America and author of several garden books.

For the past 18 years Felder has written a weekly garden column and now has a regular column on the Web. In addition, he hosts weekly radio and television shows and is a frequent guest on national television programs.

Contents

Start with the Basics

6 Soil & Plant Parts
8 Tools 'n' Stuff
10 Talk Like a Gardener
12 Safety First
13 Plant Zones

Creating Garden Spaces

16 Boot Kickin' Planter
18 Pit Stop Planter
20 Pop Goes the Planter
22 Multiplying Garden
24 Compost Machine
26 Weather Station

The Indoor Garden

30 Worm Tower
32 Jurassic Jungle
34 Rootin' Tootin' Potato
36 Desert Garden
38 Egg Heads

Into the Wild

42 Home Tweet Home
44 Birdie Breakfast
46 Bottle Cop Snake
48 Dirty Bird's Bath
50 For the Birds
52 Flutter-by Garden
54 How Does Your Gourd Grow?
56 Out of Your Gourd Birdhouse

Just Eat It!

60 Three Sisters Garden
62 Scare-dee-crow
64 Tub-O-Taters
66 Rabbit Chow
68 Flavor Garden
70 Bean Teepee
72 Teeny-Tiny Tomatoes

Flower Power

76 Roy G. Biv Garden
78 Buddy Bouquet
80 Flower Shop
82 Sunflower House

Make It Pretty

86 Wind Glove
88 Canned Music
90 Garden Lantern
92 A-mazing Path
94 Wattle Fence
96 Thing Tree
98 Anything Bench
100 Stepping Stone Jewels

Children's Resource

104 Great Kids' Gardens
107 Finding More Info
108 Great Plants for Kids

Index ☛ 110

Start with the Basics

Gardens and flowers do not just HAPPEN—they need somebody to get them started. The same goes for you—this book gets you started with garden projects—rated from easy ones you can do by yourself (Skill Scale ✿) to ones you will need help with (Skill Scale ✿✿✿). You will learn how to recognize the parts of a plant, how to make good dirt, and how to take care of what you plant. Plus, you will have fun DOING stuff—and sharing what you learn with your friends!

Soil & Plant Parts

Dirt is where wild trees and flowers grow their roots. Plain dirt is not very good for some plants, so gardeners add extra stuff to it to make it better—like stirring crumbled crackers into a bowl of soup or chili. The dirt is then called **soil**.

Plain dirt always has a little bit of plant food in it, but gardeners often add extra fertilizer to make it garden soil. Good soil holds water during dry weather but lets extra water drain during rainy seasons so plant roots do not stay too wet. **Roots** grow deep and wide in most soils, and help plants find water and food. Good strong roots are important because they help hold plants upright even in very strong winds.

Most gardeners cover the soil beneath their plants with a layer of leaves, pinestraw, hay, or bark to protect the plant roots from the sun. This layer is called **mulch** and does not have to be very deep—just deep enough to cover the soil. Worms love to eat mulch and turn it into compost. Mulch also helps keep some weed seeds from growing by shading them from the sun, which they need in order to sprout.

Plants have all sorts of parts that work together to help them grow well. Plants grow up toward the **sunlight**. Their green **leaves** turn sunlight into energy to help them grow. We love to look at flowers with their pretty **petals** and smell them, but they are even more important to the plants. Butterflies, bees, and even the wind help flowers make seeds, which grow into new plants.

Trees and shrubs have very hard stems, called **trunks**, made out of wood to help them stand up strong for years. Other plants have special roots or bulbs to help them stay alive underground during cold winters or hot summers. They will sprout back up when the weather is better for growing.

Tools 'n' Stuff

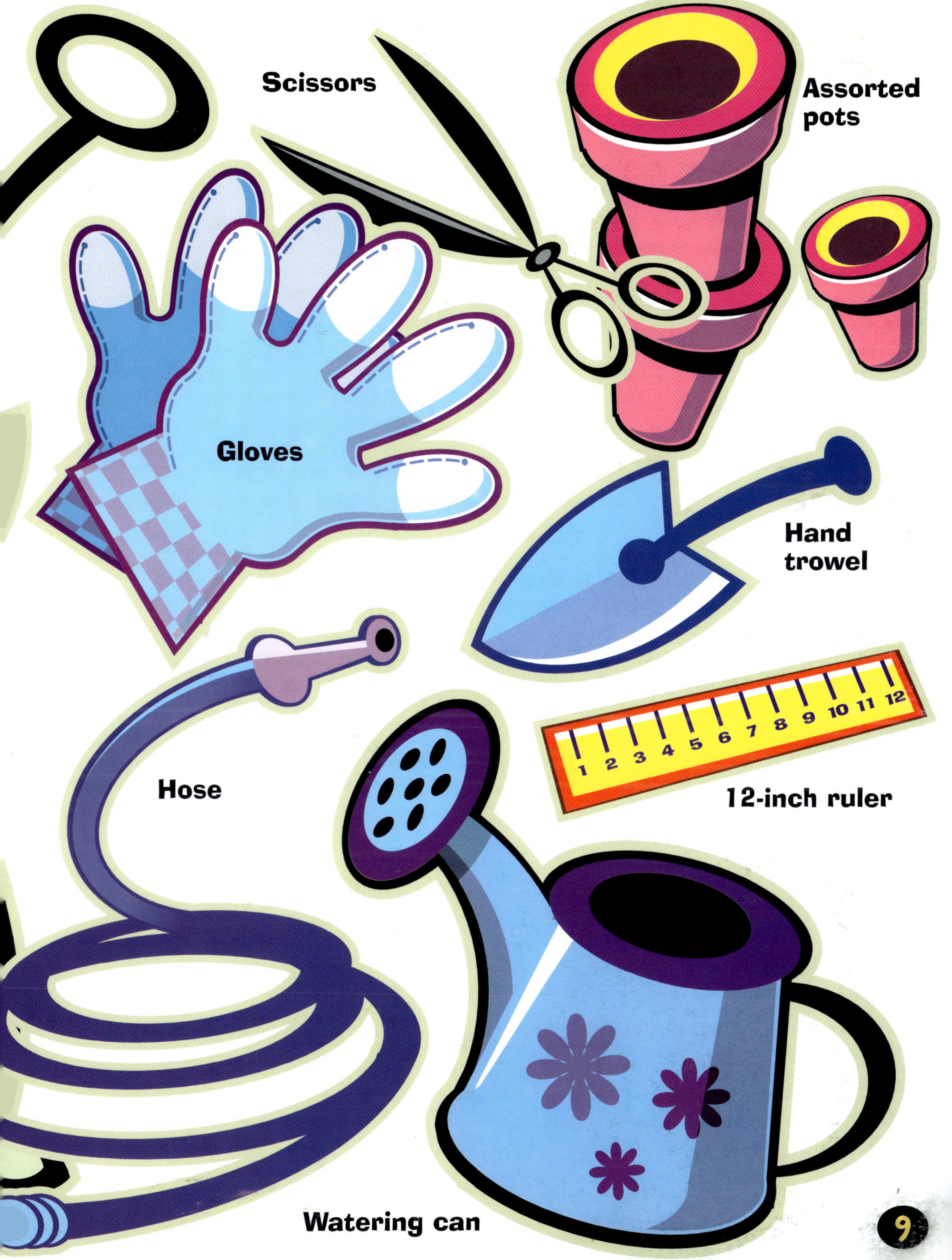
Scissors
Assorted pots
Gloves
Hand trowel
Hose
1 2 3 4 5 6 7 8 9 10 11 12
12-inch ruler
Watering can

Talk Like a Gardener

People use special words when they talk about their gardens. You may have your own words, but here are a few that will help you tell other people about your garden or ask for what you need.

Annual: a flower or vegetable that lives only part of the year.

Bulb: an underground part of some plants that sprouts leaves and flowers.

Compost: what leaves, kitchen scraps, and other waste turn into when they are piled up outside and left alone. It looks and feels like soil and helps plants grow better when added to dirt.

Container: anything that you can grow a plant in. It holds soil but has holes in the bottom to let water drain.

Dig: when you use a shovel or trowel to make a hole or mix stuff into the ground.

Dirt: what is under your house and under the grass. Trees grow roots deep into dirt, but some flowers do not grow well in just plain dirt (see page 6).

Fertilizer: extra plant food that is added to the soil or water.

Flowers: the pretty parts of a plant, made of petals, where seeds are made.

Fruit: the part of a plant that grows after the flowers and contains seed. Most fruits can be eaten by people.

Full Sun: all day sun. Many vegetables and flowers need at least half a day—6 hours—of sunshine to grow well. Full sun is hot.

Hose: a long tube used to take water from a faucet to plants.

Leaves: parts of a plant that grow on stems and turn sunlight into plant energy.

Mulch: a thin layer of leaves, pine needles, hay, or torn-up newspaper placed over the top of the ground beneath a plant's leaves, which keeps the sunshine from making garden soil too hot.

Part Shade: when the sun shines on an area for less than half a day.

Perennial: a plant that lives for many years.

Roots: the parts of a plant that grow in the ground or in water. They soak up food and water from the soil to feed the plant.

Season: the time of the year—winter, spring, summer, or fall. Some plants grow only in the spring and summer, then freeze in the fall and winter. Other plants grow in the winter, from fall to spring, and get too hot in the summer to grow very well.

Shade: the area where the sun does not shine directly on plants. Some plants will burn if planted in the sun and must have shade all day.

Shrubs: often called bushes. These are planted outside around our houses. Many shrubs have colorful flowers part of the year or pretty leaves.

Soil: dirt that has had stuff, like old leaves, compost, or sand, added to it. Many plants grow better in the new soil than they would in plain dirt.

Stem: the part of a plant that holds up leaves and flowers.

Tools: shovels, trowels, and other things you use to dig in the soil, plant seeds, and weed your garden.

Vegetables: the kinds of plants, such as corn and potatoes, that we grow to eat.

Weed: any plant that comes up by itself where you do not want it to grow.

Safety First

Have fun in the garden, and always be careful. Some things can hurt you. And sometimes it's good to ask a grown-up for help.

Love the birds, butterflies, frogs, and other wildlife (even bees) that visit your garden, but do not try to catch them or pick them up because some are afraid of people and others can bite or sting.

Birds and animals can eat things that people cannot—some plants and other garden things will make you sick if you eat them. Never put anything like fertilizer or compost in your mouth. And never eat anything—especially berries, mushrooms, bulbs, and other stuff—you aren't sure about.

Ants, worms, and broken glass can be hiding in the garden dirt. So protect your hands by wearing gloves when you are digging.

Tools are for gardening, not play. Scissors and knives can cut you, so be careful. Do not run with them or put them in your mouth. Please put all your tools away when you are not using them—someone might step on them and get hurt.

Lots of children get hurt by falling. Ask a grown-up if you need help reaching or climbing.

Try not to hurt plants. Running or kicking balls in flower or vegetable beds can break plants. Carving on tree and shrub stems can kill them.

Wear a hat in the garden to keep your head cool. A sunburn can sneak up on you, even on a cloudy day. Using sunscreen can protect you from getting too much sun.

North America is very large, and some areas get colder than others in the winter or stay hotter in the summer. Some parts—like the South or the West Coast—almost never get snow or below freezing temperatures, and gardeners there can grow things for many months. Because some areas get cold earlier and stay cold longer, gardeners in different areas do not plant at the same time. On the map, find where you live, and the best time to start planting your garden. As you garden, you will find that some plants can go into the ground earlier or later. Read the seed packets for more specific information.

Plant Zones

CREATING
GARDEN
SPACES

The word **GARDEN** means "a guarded area"—a private place. Some people put small fences around their garden to set it off from the rest of the yard and to let other people know it is a special place. Show that your garden is, too, by outlining it with rocks, bricks, or interesting pieces of wood. Make a string fence with some small sticks and a ball of twine—any kind of fence will do. Then decorate your garden any way you want!

Boot Kickin' Planter

Anything that will hold soil and let water drain can be used for growing plants. Look for plastic bottles, metal cans, buckets, used tires, garbage bags—even old boots.

You'll Need:

- Hammer
- 1 big nail
- 1 old boot (ask Mom or Dad first)
- Newspapers
- Paint
- Potting soil
- Flower seeds or a plant

HOW YOU DO IT:

1 Use the hammer and nail to punch holes in the bottom of the boot.

2 Spread out some old newspapers to keep things neat.

3 Paint the boot any way you want. Do something that will look good with your flowers.

4 Fill the boot with potting soil—poke some way into the toe.

5 Push seeds a little way into the potting soil (big seeds an inch deep, little seeds about half an inch). Or, set a plant into the boot, then cover its roots with soil.

6 Put the boot in a sunny place and water it every few days. After the plants start growing, you will need to feed them with fertilizer.

Did You Know?

Small containers like boots can dry out quickly or fall over if the plant is too big. Grow plants that stay small in them.

PIT STOP PLANTER

Little pots dry out fast outdoors. It is easier to plant lots of stuff in one large container. Why not recycle an old tire? It is easy to find, and you can paint it any way you want.

YOU'LL NEED:

- Grease remover (ask a grown-up for help)
- Water
- Garden hose
- 1 old car tire
- Newspapers
- Outdoor paint
- Paintbrushes
- Disposable gloves

HOW YOU DO IT:

1 Use grease remover and water from the garden hose to scrub the tire clean so paint will stick to it. Let the tire dry for an hour or two.

2 Spread out the newspapers several layers thick on the driveway or lawn. Cover an area as big as a bed. Put the clean, dry tire in the middle.

3 Carefully paint the tire one color and let it dry before you decorate it with pretty designs.

4 Decorate your tire with stars, hearts, stripes, circles, or any other design. Have fun, but try to paint only the tire—not yourself!

5 To make a hand design, first put a disposable glove on your hand (not the one you write with). Put that hand on the tire with your fingers spread apart. Draw or paint around your hand. Later you can paint your handprint any color you want.

HOW YOU USE IT:

When the tire is completely dry, put it flat on the ground and fill it with soil. Then plant flowers or vegetables in it. Mix different kinds of plants together. Water the plants and feed them every few weeks.

Did You Know?

Millions of tires are thrown away every year. Your tire planter will last much longer than the wooden half barrels grown-ups use. And you can repaint it anytime you want.

POP GOES THE PLANTER

Flowers and vegetables grow well in a raised bed—a garden that is built up from the ground. It warms up early in the spring sunshine and does not stay wet in heavy rains. It is also easy to plant a raised bed garden and keep it weeded.

YOU'LL NEED:

- Empty 2-liter plastic soda pop bottles (about 3 for every 1 foot of flower bed)
- Garden hose
- Shovel
- Potting soil or compost
- Food coloring (2 or 3 bottles of each color)
- Flowers from a garden center

Skill Scale

HOW YOU DO IT:

1 Measure your garden area to see how many bottles you will need.

2 Use the garden hose to outline the area where you want to make the raised bed.

3 With the shovel, dig a ditch 4 inches deep and as wide as the bottle. Put the dirt from the ditch into the middle of the bed, not on the outside.

4 Line the ditch with bottles, each one touching another. Use the hose to fill the bottles with water, then add the food coloring. Color the bottles in the same order as colors in a rainbow (see ROY G. BIV Garden on page 76).

5 Add potting soil or compost to the ditch dirt in the middle of the garden. Then mix it all together.

6 Plant seeds or flowers in the raised bed. Give them a good watering. They will need feeding when they start growing.

Did You Know?

People all over the world have gardened in raised beds for hundreds of years. You can start planting earlier in spring in a raised bed because the soil warms up faster.

MULTIPLYING GARDEN

You can grow new plants by cutting off parts of old ones and planting them in potting soil. Stems, and sometimes leaves, can grow new roots and whole new plants this way. With this kind of recycling, you get new plants for free.

YOU'LL NEED:

- Potting soil
- Sand
- Water
- Small pots
- Plants that are easy to grow from cuttings, like mother-in-law plant, coleus, jade, or philodendron
- Scissors, pruners, or sharp knife
- Plastic jugs with the bottoms cut off (ask a grown-up for help)

HOW YOU DO IT:

1 Mix potting soil and sand together (half and half). Add enough water to make it moist. Fill pots with the mixture.

2 Cut fresh pieces of stems (or leaves from the mother-in-law plant). Use a pencil to make a hole in the potting soil in each pot. Stick a cutting in the hole so half of it shows above the soil. Water to settle the soil around the cutting.

3 Put the pots in a bright place, but not in hot sunshine.

4 Cover the potted cuttings with the cut-off jugs. This keeps the air around the cuttings moist. Water every few days.

5 Cuttings may take a month or longer to make new roots. Do not tug on the plants until then or you may break off the tender new roots.

Did You Know?

Most of the shrubs, vines, and small trees that you see at garden centers were grown from cuttings just like yours.

COMPOST MACHINE

Where do leaves go after they fall from trees? Worms and other creatures that live in the ground eat them. The leaves turn into a special kind of good dirt, called compost, which feeds roots.

YOU'LL NEED:

- A place in your yard for a compost pile
- Shovel
- Bags of old leaves
- Grass clippings or weeds
- Kitchen scraps (no meat or bones) like vegetable or fruit peels, coffee grounds, leftover salad, eggshells
- Garden hose or bucket
- Water

Did You Know?
Worms are not the only things that make compost. There are "good" bacteria and fungus—too small to see—that also "eat" leaves and kitchen scraps.

HOW YOU DO IT:

1 With your shovel, mix leaves, grass clippings, weeds, and scraps together. Heap them into a big pile with a big dent in the top. Pour water in the dent to soak the pile.

2 Wait 2 or 3 days, then use the shovel to mix everything again. Pile it up and make another dent in the top. Notice how hot the mixture is getting—heat is produced as your pile decays.

3 Mix the ingredients every few days and add water to keep the pile moist. The compost is ready to use when it is dark and crumbly. This takes at least a month.

4 Use the finished compost to start seeds or to add to the soil around plants.

Weather Station

It is cool to know what the weather is—just like the TV weather person. Make a weather station that tells you what is happening in your own backyard.

You'll Need:

- 3 wooden poles about as tall as you (long sticks or broom handles will do)
- 2 pieces of heavy string, about 3 feet long
- 1 soda pop can

Did You Know?

Some kids live where the weather is nice enough to garden outside all year. Others live where the winter is cold or wet—they can garden inside.

HOW YOU DO IT:

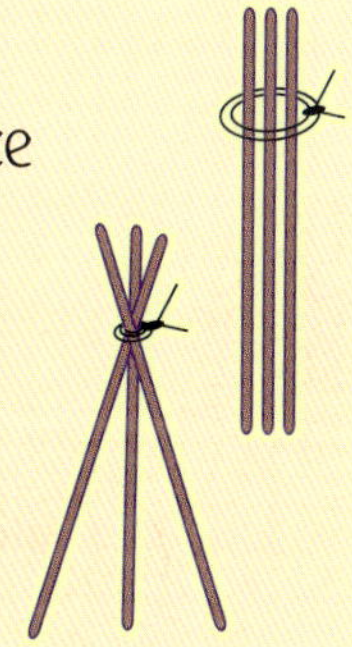

1 Lay the 3 poles down, side by side. Use 1 piece of string to tie them together at one end.

2 Stand the poles up and spread out the legs so they look like a teepee.

3 Tie one end of the second string to the top of the teepee and the other end around the can so the can hangs between the poles about halfway to the ground. Make sure the can hangs free, so it can swing around.

HOW IT WORKS:

When you go outside, touch the can. If it is wet, it must be raining—go get a raincoat. If the can is cold, snowy, or icy—put on a warm coat. If it is blowing sideways, the weather is very windy—go back inside.

THE INDOOR GARDEN

No matter where you live, sometimes the weather outside is not good for gardening—it may be too cold, too hot, or too wet. That is when indoor projects can keep you and your garden going. There are plants that grow best inside your house and neat projects you can make and enjoy without having to go outside. Some of them will even do well in your classroom at school!

WORM TOWER

There are lots of things you can do with soda pop bottles—even stack them up and fill them with wet newspaper and worms to make your own soil for growing flowers.

YOU'LL NEED:

- Scissors
- Two 2-liter plastic soda pop bottles
- Marking pen or pencil
- Ruler
- Newspapers
- 1 cup of chopped up vegetable (no meat) scraps from the kitchen
- 1 eggshell
- 1 box of red wriggler worms from a bait shop
- Potting soil
- 1 small plant from a garden center

MAKE THE TOWER:

1 Use the scissors to punch several holes in the bottom of one of the bottles. Ask a grown-up to help you.

2 Draw a line around the same bottle about 4 inches from the bottom. Cut the bottle along the line.

3 Turn the long end upside down, and place the smaller end in the top so it fits snugly. This will be your planting container.

4 Draw a line around the other bottle about 8 inches from the bottom. Cut the bottle along the line.

5 Place the first bottle inside the second bottle so the screw top faces down.

Make the Compost:

1 Tear the newspaper into very thin strips (tear from the top of the page to the bottom). Soak the strips in water for a few minutes, then let them drain well—you want them moist, not wet.

2 Chop the vegetable scraps and the eggshell into very small pieces. Mix them with the moist paper strips—about one cup of scraps to four cups of shredded paper.

3 Open the top of the bottle tower, and fill it with the paper and scrap mixture. Do not pack it tightly.

4 Gently add the worms to the paper and scraps (they will squirm down in it). Do not hurt them!

5 Put the top bottle back on the bottle tower, making sure it fits, so the worms cannot get out.

6 Fill the top of the tower with potting soil and plant your plant. Water it well.

How It Works:

Put the worm tower in a cool place inside, but not where the sun shines on it (or the worms will get hot and die). Check it every few days to make sure it is not dry. Slowly pour out any of the brownish water that collects in the bottom; use it on flowers or other plants as fertilizer water. Add more chopped vegetables in 2 or 3 weeks. The worms will eat the paper and the scraps, turning them into compost. Add the compost to potting soil or to your garden.

Jurassic Jungle

You can grow your very own jungle in your room with plants and everything! Add vines, sticks, and toy animals for a very scary (or very nice) SAFARI!

You'll Need:

- Plastic sweater box or small aquarium
- Aquarium gravel
- Potting soil
- Small ferns and other tropical plants from a garden center
- Sticks, branches, rocks
- 1 large jar cap
- Green moss
- Toy dinosaurs or other jungle animals
- Sponge
- Turkey baster

How You Do It:

1 Fill the bottom of the sweater box with 2 inches of aquarium gravel. Add 3 or 4 inches of potting soil.

2 Carefully plant the ferns and small tropical plants—some tall, some short, some vines (helpers at a garden center can help you pick some good ones).

3 Place sticks, branches, and rocks where they look natural. Bury the jar cap up to the rim and fill it with water so it looks like a pond. Carefully push patches of the green moss into bare soil.

4 Put toy dinosaurs and other jungle animals around the plants. Make it look like a real jungle.

5 Put the jungle in bright light but not where the sun shines directly on it.

Did You Know?

Tall jungle trees and vines shade smaller plants. All sorts of creatures live there—from the tree tops down to the jungle floor.

WHAT NOW?

Use a wet sponge to squeeze drops of water, like rainfall, onto the plants. Do not use too much water or the jungle soil will turn into a swamp and the plants may die! Use a turkey baster to suck up extra water that collects down in the gravel. Every month, add a little fertilizer to your water or use the liquid from the Worm Tower (see page 31).

Rootin' Tootin' Potato

Sweet potatoes—that you bake and eat with butter—grow underground on the roots of a jungle vine. Grow your own vine from a sweet potato in a jar of water on a windowsill.

You'll Need:

- 5 or 6 toothpicks
- 1 whole, uncooked sweet potato (from the grocery store)
- Drinking glass or a clear glass or plastic jar
- Water
- A bright, sunny window sill

Did You Know?
Sweet potatoes are one of the things that monkeys in zoos love to eat!

HOW YOU DO IT:

1. Stick the toothpicks around the middle of the sweet potato to hold the potato halfway out of the glass.
2. Fill the glass with water, so the bottom half of the sweet potato is in the water.
3. Put the glass on a sunny windowsill where you can see it.
4. Add water every few days to keep the bottom half of the potato submerged.

WHAT NOW?

The sweet potato will soon sprout thin white roots of its own in the water. Green stems with leaves will start growing out of the top. If you want to plant the sweet potato in your garden in the spring, plant it in a spot that will be sunny all summer. New sweet potatoes will grow from its roots.

DESERT GARDEN

You can grow one or two small plants in a goldfish bowl. Even cactus plants will grow there, if you don't water them too much!

YOU'LL NEED:

- Goldfish bowl
- Small rocks
- Colorful aquarium gravel
- Potting soil
- Small plants, like aloe, sedum, jade, or cactus (from a garden center)
- Pretty rocks and small, interesting sticks
- Sponge
- Water

HOW YOU DO IT:

1 Fill the bottom of the goldfish bowl with small rocks and a layer of aquarium gravel, about 1 inch deep.

2 Add about 2 inches of potting soil. Make little hills of soil where your plants will grow.

3 Carefully plant each of your plants in a hill of potting soil.

4 Put pretty rocks and sticks around the plants to decorate the garden and make it look like a real desert.

5 Use a wet sponge to squeeze a few drops of water at a time onto the soil around the plants until the soil gets moist.

6 Keep your garden near a window but not in hot sun.

7 Water your desert garden only when it gets very dry.

Did You Know?

Little cactus plants growing in a small goldfish bowl without a top on it only need a few drops of water about once a month.

EGG HEADS

It takes only about a week to grow a great patch of hair from grass seed planted in an egg head—you can even trim it with scissors!

YOU'LL NEED:

- Scissors
- White paper
- Paint or crayons
- Tape or glue
- 1 egg
- Potting soil
- Ryegrass or fescue grass seed
- Water

Did You Know?
Ornamental grasses are planted in the garden and are not mowed. They range from 6 inches to 10 feet tall.

How You Do It:

1 To make a stand, use scissors to cut a strip of paper 4 inches long and 1 inch wide. Tape or glue the ends. Draw a collar.

2 With a scissors, make a big hole in one end of a clean, uncooked egg. Pour out the raw egg (do not get any uncooked egg in your mouth).

3 Wash the shell. When it is dry, paint a face on it. Then set the egg head on its stand.

4 Fill the eggshell with potting soil. Sprinkle the grass seeds on top. Water gently.

5 Watch the grass grow. Give it a haircut when the grass gets too tall.

Into the Wild

Birds and spiders and bees—oh my! All sorts of wild creatures live in your yard and garden. The more kinds of plants you have, the greater the variety of critters that will make their home with you. Lots of different insects and animals make your garden healthy—by eating pests, improving soil, or making fertilizer. They also make your yard a more beautiful and interesting place. You can do many things to attract birds and good creatures to your yard.

Home Tweet Home

Most wild birds build nests in trees with twigs and leaves. You can make a simple house that birds will want to move into.

You'll Need:

- Scissors
- 1 coffee can with a snap-on lid
- Hammer
- 1 large nail
- 1 wire coat hanger
- Rubber bands
- Lots of twigs that are longer than the coffee can
- 4-foot piece of vine

How You Do It:

1 Cut a hole in the plastic coffee can lid—near one edge and about 2 inches around.

2 Hammer a hole in the bottom of the can with the nail near the edge (you may need a grown-up's help).

3 Put the plastic lid on the coffee can so the hole in the lid lines up with the hole in the bottom of the can.

4 Straighten the coat hanger. Push it through the holes in the can and the lid. Bend and twist the ends together so you can hang the birdhouse from a tree limb.

Skill Scale

5 Use rubber bands to hold the twigs in place all around the can. Put in a long twig for birds to use as a perch.

6 Wrap the vine around the birdhouse to hide the rubber bands. Hang it in a tree or shrub.

Try this one too!

Toad House

1 In a flower bed near the house, dig a small hole deep enough to plant a daylily plant and a 6-inch clay pot side by side.

2 Bury the clay pot on its side, with only a little of it showing. Plant the daylily close to the open end of the pot.

3 A toad, which will eat mosquitoes and slugs, can make its home in the cool pot.

Birdie Breakfast

Put a bird feeder near your home and watch colorful wild birds flock to it. They will bring their families and friends, and you will see their many shapes, colors, types of feathers and beaks, different ways they act, and sounds they make.

You'll Need:

- Hammer
- 1 big nail
- 1 clear plastic bottle with a screw-on top
- 2 small twigs, about as long as the bottle
- Paint (optional)
- 1 small nail
- 1 piece of wire, about 1 foot long
- Birdseed

How You Do It:

1 With the hammer and big nail, punch four holes about one-half inch from the bottom of the bottle, one on each side of the bottle. The holes should be as big around as the twigs.

2 Make four more holes, each one about 1 inch above the first four holes.

3 Push the twigs through the bottom holes so they stick out evenly on each side of the bottle. These are the perches the birds stand on when they feed.

4 Draw "eyes" around the top holes if you want. This makes the feeder prettier, but birds will still come and eat even if you choose not to.

5 With the small nail, punch two holes in the bottle, one on each side, right below where the cap screws on.

6 Push the wire through the top holes and twist the ends together.

7 Fill the bottle with birdseed, and screw on the cap. Hang the feeder near your house—you can even watch the birds from inside in the winter.

Did You Know? There are lots of different birdseeds, but you can attract many kinds of birds, from chickadees to woodpeckers, with one bird food—sunflower seeds!

Bottle Cap Snake

Some critters, like mice, can harm your garden by nibbling on plants or their roots. But, you might be able to scare them away with a lifelike snake to police your garden space.

You'll Need:

- About 150 metal bottle caps
- Hammer
- 2 nails—1 large and 1 small
- Handsaw
- Old broomstick
- Sharp knife
- Heavy wire, 3 feet long
- Green and brown paint
- 2 thumbtacks

Skill Scale ✿✿✿

How You Do It:

1 Set the bottle caps, one at a time, on a hard surface. Use the hammer and big nail to punch a hole in the middle of each one.

2 Get a grown-up to help saw two 3-inch pieces off the broomstick. Use the knife to carve a pointed tail and round head (get a grown-up to help).

3 Use the small nail to punch a hole in the cut ends of the tail and head.

4 Push one end of the wire into the hole in the tail. String the bottle caps, with the bottom of the caps facing the tail.

5 When all the caps are strung on the wire, cut off all but 1 inch of extra wire. Push the snake head onto the end.

6 Paint the snake green and brown. Use the thumbtacks as eyes. You may want to decorate your snake—cut out a paper or cloth tongue and glue it on.

Dirty Bird's Bath

Birds love to take splashy baths! They cannot swim, so they look for water they can stand up in. You can make a perfect birdbath that butterflies will enjoy, too.

You'll Need:

- 5 sturdy sticks, about 4 feet long
- Rope or wire, about 6 feet long
- 18-inch plastic flowerpot saucer
- Rocks about the size of your fist

Skill Scale

How You Do It:

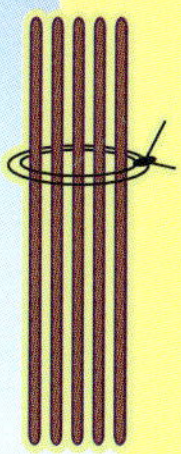

1 Lay the sticks down side by side. Use the rope to tie them together tightly in the middle.

2 Find a sunny area away from shrubs (where bird-eating cats hide).

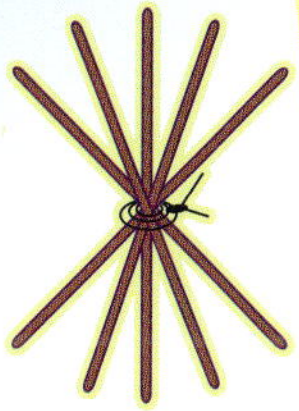

3 Stand up the sticks and spread them apart to make a teepee.

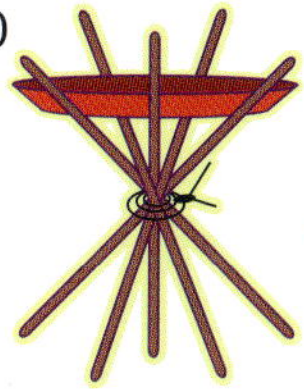

4 Place the saucer in the "nest" at the top. Make sure it is level so the water will not spill out.

5 Fill the saucer with water. Set the rocks around in the water to give birds and butterflies a place to perch.

6 Check it every few days and give the birds fresh, clean water.

Did You Know? Butterflies need water, too. They like shallow water and warm rocks. Place rocks in a shallow birdbath for them to perch while they drink.

For the Birds

Turn your garden into a supermarket for birds! Hang different kinds of food and nest-making supplies in your shrubs and trees to make your garden a one-stop shop.

You'll Need:

- Spoon and small knife
- Orange halves
- String or ribbon for hanging
- Birdseed
- Mixing bowl
- Peanut butter
- Solid shortening or lard
- Pinecones
- Mesh bags (like the ones onions come in)
- Dryer lint and bits of thread and yarn

How You Do It:

1 With a spoon, scoop out the orange halves—do not break the peel. Use the knife to poke three holes (evenly spaced) around the edge of the peel.

2 Tie one piece of string through each hole. Tie all three strings together at the top. Fill the basket with birdseed.

3 In a bowl, mix equal amounts of peanut butter and shortening. Then mix in lots of birdseed until it looks like the picture (see page 51).

4 Tie a string or ribbon on a pinecone so it can be hung. Roll the pinecone in the peanut butter and birdseed mix.

5 Stuff the mesh bag with dryer lint and short pieces of thread and yarn.

6 Hang all three of these projects high in trees and shrubs where birds can find them.

Did You Know? You can attract lots of different kinds of birds by mixing big and little seeds with raisins and chopped grapes.

Flutter-by Garden

Butterflies are pretty but not very smart. Sometimes they need to be shown the way to your garden. Homemade butterfly ornaments may attract the REAL ones to your flowers.

You'll Need:

- Scissors
- Scraps of colorful fabric
- Wooden clothespins
- Marking pens or paint in bright colors

Skill Scale

How You Do It:

1 Cut out bow tie shapes (like fat figure-eights) 4 inches by 6 inches from the scraps of fabric.

2 Take two of the shapes; lay one on top of the other. Scrunch them together in the middle.

3 Use a clothespin as a butterfly body to hold the wings together.

4 Color or paint the body. Draw eyes. (You can glue on doll's eyes and pipe cleaner antennae.)

5 Clip your "flutter-bys" on shrubs and flowers where real butterflies can see them.

Flowers that Butterflies LOVE

- Ageratum
- Buddleia (butterfly bush)
- Cosmos
- Lantana **(Warning: DO NOT eat the berries!)**
- Phlox
- Queen Anne's lace
- Zinnia

Did You Know? Butterflies love naturally sweet fruit. Put a slice of watermelon or banana out in an open area and watch the butterflies come to it!

How Does Your Gourd Grow?

A gourd is a fast-growing vine. The vine makes big, hard-shelled fruits that you can decorate or use as birdhouses. Plant the seeds in spring, and harvest the gourds in fall.

You'll Need:

- A sunny garden spot
- A wire fence, trellis, or teepee that vines can grow up
- Different kinds of gourd seed (find at garden centers or in mail-order catalogs)
- Compost and fertilizer
- Scissors

How You Do It:

1 Find a place in the sun beside a wire fence, trellis, or tall teepee.

2 Dig planting holes about 2 feet wide and 1 foot deep. Mix in two shovels of compost and 1 tablespoon of fertilizer with the dirt and put the mixture back in the hole.

3 Plant five or six gourd seeds 1 inch deep. Cover with soil, then water well.

4 When the vines sprout, use the scissors to snip off all but one or two in each area so they will have lots of room to grow.

5 Let the vines grow up the support any way they want to.

6 Water well once every two weeks. Gourds do not need much water.

Now What?

When the gourds get hard, usually in late summer or early fall, cut them off the vines with scissors. Leave a couple of inches of stem on the gourd. After you have cut them off the vine, put the gourds in a warm, dry place for a week or two so the outside will get harder.

Did You Know? Native Americans used gourds to carry water, medicine, food, and seeds. They also made them into bowls, spoons, and musical instruments.

Out of Your Gourd Birdhouse

For centuries, people have made birdhouses out of gourds. They are easy to make and birds like to live in them—even if they look like giant earrings for trees.

You'll Need:

- Water
- 1 large, dried gourd
- 1 big nail
- Sharp knife
- Ruler
- Flexible wire, about 2 feet long

How You Do It:

1 Wash and clean the gourd. Scrub it smooth.

2 Use the nail to scratch three holes in the bottom of the gourd (to let out rain water). Do not use a hammer, or the gourd will break!

3 Use the nail to make two small holes near the top of the gourd (to run the wire through for hanging the gourd).

4 To begin making the door, use the nail to lightly scratch a hole in the side of the gourd.

5 Carefully use the sharp knife to make the door hole bigger, a little at a time, until the hole is about 2½ inches across. Make it smooth. Be careful not to cut yourself or crack the gourd! ASK A GROWN-UP FOR HELP.

6 Push the wire through the holes at the top. Twist the ends together to form a hanger.

7 Ask a grown-up to help you hang the birdhouse in an open area.

Did You Know? Purple martin birds nest in gourds. Some people think purple martins eat lots of mosquitoes, but they do not. They eat wasps and dragonflies.

Just Eat It

Gardening is more than just flowers and fun. It is FOOD, too! The first gardens that people in ancient times made were just for growing food. You can plant seeds that grow into many of your favorite fruits, vegetables, and herbs—just like gardeners have done for thousands of years.

Three Sisters Garden

Native Americans called corn, beans, and squash the three sisters because they grew so well together. Each one helps the other. You can grow this family in your own garden.

You'll Need:

- A small, sunny garden, about 3 feet across
- Shovel
- Compost or potting soil
- ½ cup of dry garden fertilizer
- 5 or 6 seeds of any kind of squash, 10 or 12 climbing bean seeds, and 10 or 12 corn seeds
- Water
- Scissors
- Sunflower seeds (optional)

How You Do It:

1 In an area about 3 feet across, use a shovel to mix 2 gallons of compost or potting soil and ½ cup of fertilizer with your garden dirt. Mound the soil mixture into a hill.

2 Plant the squash seeds in the middle of the hill, the bean seeds a few inches from the edge, and the corn in between.

3 Gently water the area every two or three days until the plants sprout, and once a week after that.

4 When the plants sprout, there may be too many for all of them to grow well. Use scissors to snip off all but one plant every 6 or 8 inches. You should have two or three squash plants, four or five corn plants, and six or seven bean plants—all growing together.

5 If you like, you can add in four or five sunflower seeds with the corn. Sunflowers are pretty and make seeds that you can eat or feed to the birds.

Did You Know?
Native Americans buried fish in their gardens. The fish slowly turned into rich plant food.

Scare-dee-crow!

A scarecrow is an easy thing to create for your garden. Dress it to look like you or someone you like. It may not scare away birds, but it will make your garden look great!

You'll Need:

- 1 wire coat hanger
- Wooden broomstick or mop handle
- Tape
- 1-quart-size plastic jug
- Waterproof markers
- An old shirt, scarf, hat, and ribbons

How You Do It:

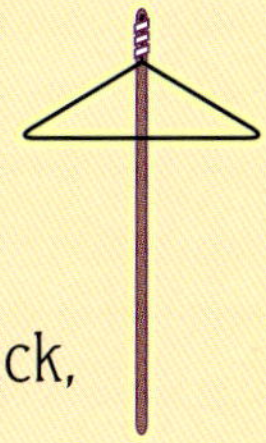

1 Straighten the curved neck of the coat hanger. Tape the coat hanger to the top of the broomstick, right-side up.

2 Push the jug "head" over the scarecrow "neck" and draw a face.

3 Dress it with a long-sleeve shirt. Add a scarf and hat. Tie ribbons on the sleeve ends to wave and flap in the wind.

4 Stand the scarecrow in a flower bed or vegetable garden.

Did You Know?

Long before Pocahontas, Native American children spent all summer in their gardens. They scared away crows by clapping their hands.

Tub-O Taters

Potatoes grow underground, but they are not roots. They grow on the buried stems of potato plants. Potatoes are very easy to grow, even in a trash can full of leaves or compost!

You'll Need:

- Knife
- 2 or 3 potatoes
- Newspapers
- Medium-sized plastic trash can
- 2 or 3 buckets of potting soil
- ½ cup of dry garden fertilizer
- 5 or 6 buckets of mulch (leaves, pine straw, or hay)

How You Do It:

1 Use the knife to cut the potatoes in half. Let them dry on some newspaper indoors for two or three days.

2 Carefully cut five ro six small holes in the bottom of the trash can. Find a sunny place outside for the trash can.

3 Mix the potting soil and fertilizer, then put the mixture in the trash can. Set the potato pieces on the potting soil. Cover them with about 6 inches of mulch. Water well.

4 Water once a week and check for new growth.

5 When the plants poke through the mulch, add 6 more inches of mulch. Repeat this as the plants grow, so only a few leaves show at a time.

Now What?

As the plants grow upwards, potatoes form on the stems. When the plants reach the top of the trash can, water once a week until the plants start to turn yellow. Then gently tip the can over and roll out the potatoes that have grown in the mulch. You can cook them and eat them any way you like!

Did You Know?

Potatoes are native to America. They became one of the most important foods in the rest of the world when Christopher Columbus took them back to Spain and Europe.

Rabbit Chow

Some people say salads are rabbit food—because rabbits like to eat greens and carrots. If you grow your own special mix, it might be fun to eat—or to feed to a rabbit.

You'll Need:

- Seeds for 5 or 6 kinds of lettuce—different colors and shapes
- 1 resealable plastic bag
- 4 plastic pots, about 6 inches across
- Potting soil
- Water
- Seeds for short, round carrots (find at garden centers or in mail-order catalogs)
- Plastic wrap
- Liquid plant food
- A sunny garden space

How You Do It:

1 Mix the lettuce seeds together in a resealable plastic bag.

2 Fill pots with potting soil and water them well.

3 Sprinkle a few carrot seeds in two pots. Sprinkle the lettuce seed mix in two pots. Save some seeds to plant later. Cover each pot with plastic wrap. Put the pots in a bright place, but not in the sun. Store any leftover lettuce seed in a cool, dry place indoors.

4 When the tiny plants start to grow, remove the plastic. Move the pots into a sunny spot outside.

5 Check the plants every day or two to see if they are getting dry and need more water.

6 Use liquid plant food every two weeks.

Did You Know?

Leafy green vegetables are very important for healthy eating. They are more fun to eat when you mix them with bits of bread, grated cheese, and your favorite salad dressing.

Now What?

It takes a while for the carrots to grow big enough to eat. You can eat the lettuce as soon as it is 3 or 4 inches tall. Use scissors to harvest the lettuce—snipping off all but an inch of the plant. It will regrow in a few weeks.

Flavor Garden

Herbs are special plants with leaves that smell and taste good. They are used to flavor food and to make tea. You can grow them in your garden or in pots on a windowsill.

You'll Need:

- Plastic pots (at least 4 inches across)
- Potting soil
- Water
- Fertilizer
- Herb plants—culinary ones such as basil, chives, mint, parsley, oregano, rosemary, sage, thyme (available from other gardeners or at garden centers)
- A sunny garden space

How You Do It:

1 If you're using pots, fill them with potting soil. If you are planting herbs in a garden, dig the soil in a sunny spot.

2 Gently loosen the roots of the herb plants. Plant them in the soil, or in pots, and cover their roots with soil.

3 Water small plants two or three times the first week after you plant them. After that, wait until they are dry before you water them again. For some herb plants, too much water is as bad as not enough water.

4 Give them a little bit of fertilizer every month—follow directions, or get a grown-up to help.

5 Pinching makes herbs grow better! As the plants grow, pinch off the tip of each branch and it will grow more branches. Use what you pinch off to flavor a salad.

Did You Know?

Some people say the word herb with the "h"—like when they say history or house. Others say it without the "h" so it sounds like "erb." No matter how you say it, they still smell and taste great!

How You Use Herbs:

- Rub the stems and leaves with your hand whenever you walk by the plants.
- Enjoy how herbs smell after you water them or after a rain.
- Sprinkle chopped leaves of basil, parsley, oregano, rosemary, sage, or thyme on pizza.
- Stir the leaves in soups or stews.
- Cut leafy stems to dry indoors. Tie a bunch together with a bow and hang upside down in your room.

Bean Teepee

Most beans grow on vines that need to climb. A chain-link fence or a bare evergreen tree can work. Make a teepee for bean vines—and you can play inside it.

You'll Need:

- A sunny garden space, about 6 feet across
- Heavy string or a piece of wire
- 5 poles, 6 feet long
- Shovel
- Dry fertilizer
- Bean seeds (try several kinds)
- Water
- Scissors

How You Do It:

1. Use heavy string or wire to tie the poles together near one end. Stand them up like a teepee.

2. Use a shovel to dig a hole the size of a dinner plate beside each pole. Mix ¼ cup of fertilizer with the dirt and refill the hole with the mixture.

3. Plant 3 or 4 bean seeds 1 inch deep by each pole. Water well.

4. When the vines come up, use scissors to snip all but one or two strong vines. Let the vines grow up the poles.

5 Feed the beans every 3 or 4 weeks. You can use the fertilizer water from the Worm Tower (see page 30) or any other plant food that is made for vegetables.

6 It will take a long time for the vines to make beans. Water every week and enjoy your teepee all summer—and even after the vines have died in the winter.

Did You Know?

Vines grow around poles one way in North America, but the other way in South America because of how the Sun shines on them and the direction the Earth spins.

Teeny-Tiny Tomatoes

Long ago, people thought tomatoes were poison and did not eat them. Now we know better and use them for many of our favorite foods—from pizza and spaghetti sauce to ketchup.

You'll Need:

- A sunny spot outside
- 1 medium-sized pot (at least 12 inches across)
- Potting soil
- 1 "patio" type tomato plant (if you cannot find one, ask a grown-up to order seeds and grow one for you)
- Water
- Mulch
- Fertilizer

How You Do It:

1 In a sunny spot outside (or a space on your deck or porch) fill the pot with potting soil. Leave room for the tomato plant.

2 With your hands, make a hole in the potting soil big enough for the roots of the tomato plant.

3 Take the tomato plant out of the pot it came in. Plant it in the hole and cover the roots with soil.

4 Water the plant. Then cover the soil with mulch 1 or 2 inches deep.

5 Water the tomato twice a week. Feed with fertilizer—follow directions or get a grown-up to help with this.

Now What?

Tomato plants produce little groups of yellow flowers. When the flowers fall off, you will see tiny tomatoes. Watch them as they grow and start to change color. A plant will grow new flowers and tomatoes for a long time. Eat tomatoes right off the plant when they are red (unless they are a yellow or other-colored tomato).

Flower Power

Flowers come in every color of the rainbow and make gardens beautiful. Use these colors to make YOUR garden the most interesting place in the world. Then, you can share its wonder with your family and special friends.

PEAS
NOW!

Roy G. Biv Garden

Roy G. Biv is a name that tells you the colors of the rainbow and their order: R-ed, O-range, Y-ellow, G-reen, B-lue, I-ndigo, and V-iolet. Learn the name and you will always remember.

You'll need:

- 7 clear plastic bottles
- Water
- Liquid food coloring
- Flowers from your garden

How you do it:

1. Fill each bottle with water.
2. Add drops of food coloring to the water—one color to each bottle to make the "Roy G. Biv" colors.
3. You can make any of the colors you do not have by following the directions on the food coloring box. Add one drop of food coloring at a time.
4. Put flowers that match the color in each bottle of colored water. Put them in a sunny place, indoors or outside, to show off their color.
5. When not using the bottles of colored water, cap them tightly to use later.

Did You Know?

When you put the stem of a white flower into a bottle of colored water, the flower slowly soaks up the color. Can you explain why this happens?

Buddy Bouquet

Sharing your flowers can give you the best feeling! You can surprise very special people by hanging a homemade basket—filled with YOUR flowers—on their doorknobs.

You'll need:

- Hammer
- 1 big nail
- 1 metal can (soup-can size)
- Paint
- Scissors
- Pretty flower pictures
- Glue or tape
- Piece of ribbon or string about 1 foot long
- Water
- Flowers with long stems cut from your garden

How you do it:

1. Use the hammer and nail to carefully punch one hole on each side of the can near the top.
2. Paint pretty designs on the can. Or, use scissors to cut out flower pictures and tape or glue them onto the can.
3. Tie each end of the ribbon through the holes to make a handle.
4. Fill the can halfway with water. Put your flowers in it to make a nice bouquet.
5. Hang the bouquet on the doorknob of a special person as a sweet surprise.

Did You Know?

Cut flowers last longer if you put the stems in water right away. It also helps to pick off any leaves in a bouquet that are below the water.

FLOWER SHOP

Flowers that look pretty in the garden can look as nice when you bring them inside. It is easy to put them together in fun and colorful ways like the people in flower shops do.

YOU'LL NEED:

- Plastic bucket
- Water
- Scissors
- Flowers from your garden
- Newspapers
- Knife
- 1 potato
- Plastic drinking straws (flexible ones if you have them)

Did You Know?

Flower shop people put flowers together with big, tall, round flowers in front and taller thin flowers in back. This is called a flower arrangement.

HOW YOU DO IT:

1 Fill the bucket halfway with water. Use scissors to cut different kinds of flowers (with stems that are at least 4 inches long). Put each flower in the water as you cut it.

2 Spread newspapers on a table. With a knife, cut a potato in half lengthwise. Put the potato cut side down on the newspaper.

3 Use scissors to cut some of the straws in half. Stick the straws into the potato, with the tall straws in the back and short ones in front.

4 Fill each straw with water and stick a flower in each one.

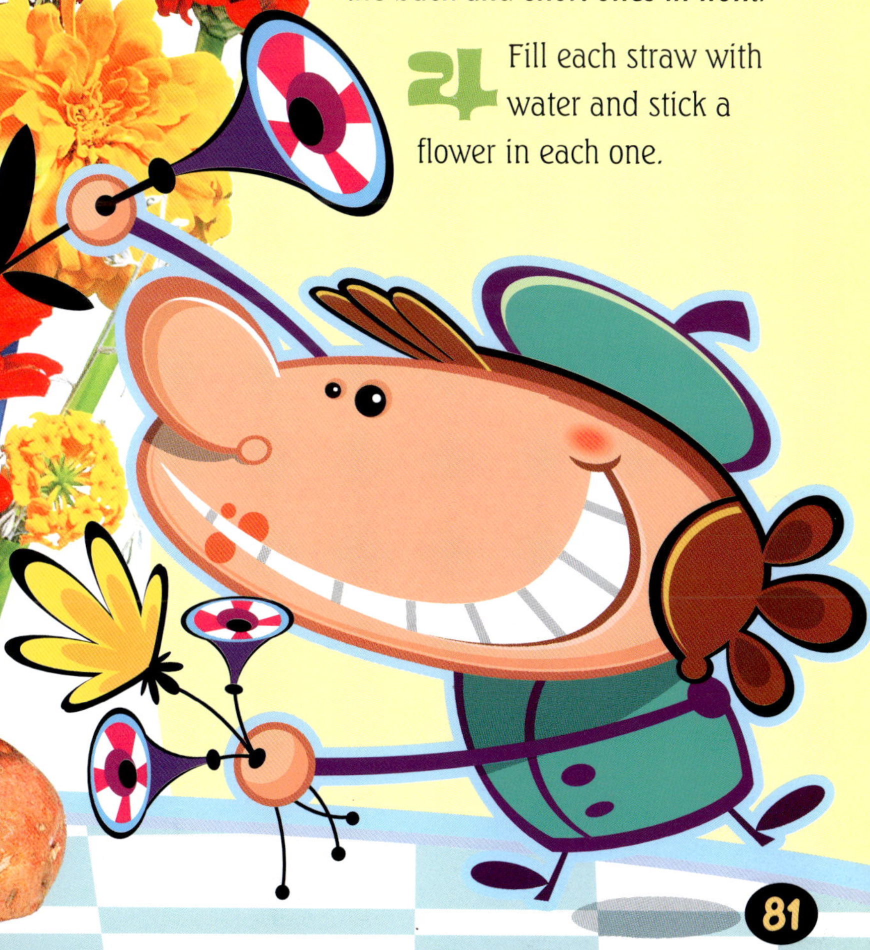

Sunflower House

Everyone needs a special, private place to go. With some seeds, a little planning, and some planting, you can grow your own! You will have one of the coolest places in your neighborhood.

You'll need:

- 9 bamboo stakes or sticks that are taller than you
- Shovel
- Sunflower seeds (the tall kinds) and morning glory seeds (you can mix different kinds if you like)
- A ball of string
- Water

How you do it:

1. In a sunny spot, stick four of the stakes in the ground, about 6 or 8 feet apart, to make the corners of a square. Stick two stakes in the ground about 2 feet apart on one side of the square to form a doorway. Stick the other three stakes in the middle of each of the other sides.

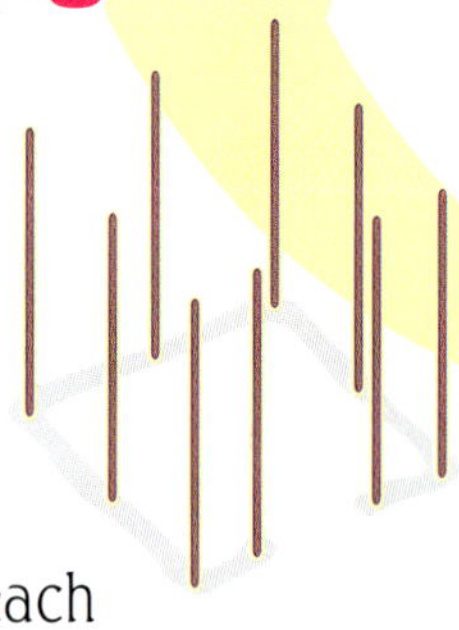

2. Use the shovel to loosen the soil around the edge of the square (but not in the doorway)—1 foot wide and one shovel deep. Ask friends or a grown-up for help.

3. Plant all the seeds about 1 inch deep along the dug-up edge. Water the planted area.

Skill Scale

4 Use the string to tie the stakes together near the ground. Start at one side of the doorway and go all the way around the house to the other side. Do this again halfway up and once more near the top of the stakes.

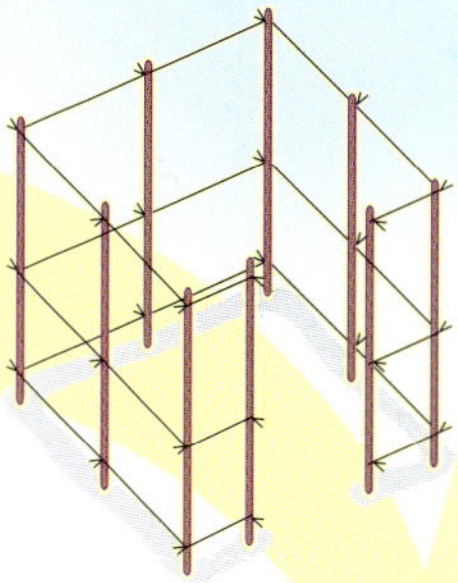

5 The sunflowers and morning glories will grow together to make a wall.

Did You Know?

Some people plant lines of shrubs close together to make a garden wall called a hedge.

Make It Pretty

Garden fun starts with what you see. All good gardens have some kind of decorations, called art. You can make garden art that shows what you think or how you feel in your garden. No two people make art the same way, and not everyone likes all kinds of art. The important thing is to make something that is fun. After all, if you cannot have fun in your own garden, where CAN you?

Wind Glove

On the hottest days of summer, you can see a breeze as it moves through the shrubs and flowers. Make something that shows even the lightest wind that blows in your garden.

You'll Need:

- 1 old garden glove (light colored if you can find one)
- Newspapers
- Colored waterproof pens
- Scissors
- 10 feet of narrow ribbon
- Hot glue gun or needle and heavy thread
- 5 shirt buttons
- 3 pieces of string about 1 foot long

How You Do It:

1. Lay the glove flat, palm down, on newspapers spread out on a table.
2. Use colored pens to draw a flower, butterfly, star, face, or other shape on the back of the glove.
3. Cut the ribbon into five 2-foot lengths
4. Use the glue gun, or a needle and thread, to attach a button on each finger of the glove, right where a fingernail would be.
5. Tie one of the 2-foot lengths of ribbon around each of the buttons to make two streamers hang from each finger.
6. Tie one end of all three pieces of string together. Attach the other end of each piece of string to the wristcuff of the glove with glue or thread. Space the pieces evenly around the cuff. This makes a hanger for the glove.
7. Hang the glove so the fingers point down and the streamers blow in the wind.

Did You Know?

People used to believe that wind socks could scare away bad spirits from the garden. These days, they might scare away crows.

Canned Music

Would you like to hear the wind? You can make a wind chime with flat parts that catch the wind and then hit one another and make musical (or clanky) sounds.

You'll Need:

- 3 sturdy branches or sticks, about 1 foot long
- Scissors
- Heavy string or wire, about 20 feet
- Newspapers
- 8 empty aluminum cans
- Spray paint

How You Do It:

1 Lay the branches in a triangle shape. Cut pieces of string to tie the ends of the branches together.

2 Cut three pieces of string 2 feet long. Tie one end of each string to a corner of the triangle. Bring the loose ends together and tie them. Hang the triangle where you can reach it.

3 Place the cans on newspapers. Spray paint the cans and let them dry.

4 Bend the tabs of each can up (do not remove them).

5 Cut six pieces of string 1 foot long. Tie an end of each string around each tab.

6 Tie a string to each corner of the triangle and one in the center of each branch. Tie each can at a different height. Each must be able to touch antother one as it moves in the wind.

7 Cut two pieces of string 2 feet long. Tie one end of each string to the tab of each of the last two cans.

8 Lay the cans on their sides on the ground and stomp them flat.

9 Tie the other end of the string of each flattened can onto the triangle so they hang below the other cans. They will catch the wind.

10 Hang the wind chime where the wind can blow on it.

Did You Know?

Most people use wind chimes for their pleasant sounds, not to detect wind. It reminds them of the beauty of nature just outside their door.

Garden Lantern

A long time ago, people used torches to light their walkways so visitors could see their way safely to their doors at night. You can make safer, colorful garden lanterns in glass jars.

You'll Need:

- Votive candles
- Small glass jars
- 2 small pitchers of water
- Orange and yellow food coloring
- Long matches

CAUTION: Adult supervision is needed anytime you work with matches or fire.

Did You Know?

A candle in a jar will not blow out, even in a strong wind, because the air pressure inside the jar is greater than that outside.

How You Do It:

1. Set a candle in each glass jar.
2. Add a few drops of food coloring to each pitcher of water.
3. Slowly pour colored water into each jar until the candle floats.
4. Ask an adult to light the candles. Use a long match to prevent burned fingers.
5. Place these lanterns so they will not burn anything and will not get broken or knocked over.

A-mazing Path

Turn your lawn into an adventure! Here is a creative project that will have your family and friends twisting and turning.

You'll Need:

- Pencil and paper
- A flat area of lawn, about 20 feet across, that needs to be mowed
- Heavy white string, at least 100 feet long that can be cut into pieces
- Scissors
- Lawn mower (get a grown-up or older kid to help with this)
- Rake

How You Do It:

1 Practice drawing a labyrinth on paper (see the drawings on page 93).

2 Lay out a labyrinth on the lawn, using string to make the lines and to connect the dots. Use scissors to cut the string as long as each line needs to be. Make the space between the lines 3 feet wide.

Did You Know?

A maze has several turns where you can decide which way to go, right or wrong. A labyrinth is one long curving line that leads you to a center. You just relax while walking or running it.

3 To make a path, have someone mow the grass between the string lines.

4 Rake the path clean, pushing the cut grass against the line "walls."

5 Take your time walking the path. Relax awhile when you are in the middle.

6 Some people take small toys or special gifts to leave in the center of a labyrinth for the next person to find.

How to Draw a Labyrinth

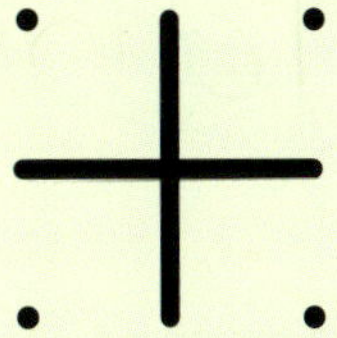

1 Make a cross in a box with a dot in each corner.

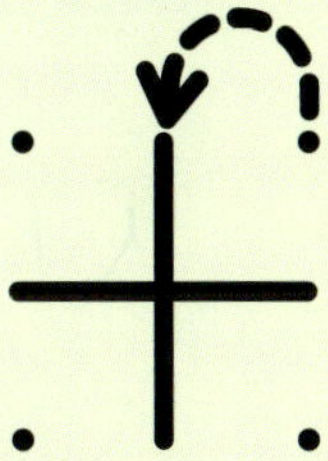

2 Connect the top right dot with the top of the cross.

3 Connect the right side of the cross with the top left dot.

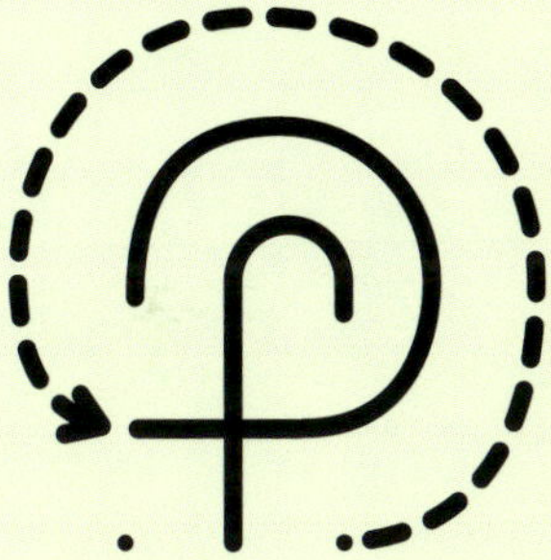

4 Connect the right bottom dot and the left side of the cross.

5 Connect the bottom of the cross with the last dot.

Wattle Fence

Anyone can weave this old-fashioned fence. The more time you spend working on it, the better it will look and the longer it will last. Be creative with the materials you use!

You'll Need:

- Hammer
- Posts, broom handles, or sturdy sticks—you need 1 post for every 1 foot of fence
- Flexible weaving materials—vines, young twigs, strips of fabric, or long grasses
- String or flexible wire for tying down loose ends
- Decorations, like strips of fabric, old shoelaces, and plastic flowers

How You Do It:

1 Use the hammer to pound the posts into the ground so they are stable. Put in a post every 1 foot. You may need help with this.

2 Work from the ground up to weave the fence. Put one end of a vine or flexible limb against the first post and bend it so it goes in the opposite direction by the second post. Bend it again and make it go again on the opposite sides of the post.

3 Keep your weaving as tight as you can. Continue to weave, adding decorations as you go.

4 Make your fence as tall as you want. A wattle fence is a pretty edge to a garden.

Did You Know?
wattle fences are still very popular in England and look very nice as a background to a secret garden.

Thing Tree

Every garden needs a THING TREE. Think yard jewelry. You can change what you hang with the seasons or have it the same all year long. Watch how the sun and the rain make it sparkle!

You'll Need:

- A sense of humor
- Shovel
- Any kind of dead tree that has lots of branches and twigs
- Colorful small bottles and jars

How You Do It:

1 Use the shovel to dig a hole about 1 foot deep, but not too wide.

2 Stand the tree up in the hole. Pack the dirt back around the tree and stomp on the dirt until the tree is steady.

3 Carefully slip bottles and jars over the ends of the branches.

4 You can dress up your tree even more using anything that is colorful and fun. Try plastic beads, tinsel, ribbons, dolls, and even flutter-bys (see page 52). You can also decorate your tree for Halloween and other holidays.

Did You Know?

Some people hung bottles near their doors to catch any bad spirits flying by at night, trapping them so the morning sunshine would destroy them.

Anything Bench

You cannot sit in your garden if there is no place to sit! Make a fun bench to put in the summer shade or the warm winter sun. You can move it anywhere you want!

You'll Need:

- Newspapers
- 2 "anythings" that are about 15 inches high and flat on the top (storage crates, concrete blocks, flat rocks, or pieces of a tree trunk that has been cut down)
- 1 wooden board that is 2 inches thick, 8 or 10 inches wide, and 4 or 5 feet long (from a wood scrap pile, or get a grown-up to help find one at a lumberyard)
- Outdoor paint, all colors
- Paintbrushes

How You Do It:

1 Spread newspapers on the driveway or the grass where you do not want paint to splash.

2 Set the two "anythings" on the newspapers and paint them. You can use one color or as many different colors as you like.

3 If the board is dirty, clean it and get rid of any splinters.

4 Lay the board across the "anythings" and paint it on one side. Let it dry. Then turn the board over and paint the other side and the edges.

5 Make designs by laying tree leaves or other patterns over the wood before painting.

Did You Know?

Wooden boards have an "up" side. Look at one end of a board, and see which way the little "rings" go. Lay the board so the rings curve up and back down like a rainbow. This keeps rain from making the board crack.

Stepping Stone Jewels

Most yards—at home or at school—have a low spot that stays wet. Fix the problem and make a work of art at the same time using some of your favorite stuff.

You'll Need:

- 60-pound bag of ready-to-mix concrete (from a building supply store)
- Wheelbarrow or large bucket for mixing
- 1 gallon of water
- Shovel or hoe
- Pizza box
- Coins, marbles, comb, rocks, pieces of broken tiles or dishes—anything small and hard you can press into wet concrete

Try making these in different shapes, using different boxes and containers for molds. Have your friends or classmates help make enough of these for an entire walkway.

Did You Know?
This ancient type of artwork is used to make pottery, sculptures, and other folk-art garden ornaments.

How You Do It:

Special Note: Concrete is heavy, so get help picking it up and mixing it with water. It can also cause a skin rash, so wear gloves and a mask when working with the mixture.

1 Carefully open and pour the bag of concrete in the wheelbarrow. Slowly stir in the gallon of water. Use the shovel or the hoe to mix. Do not add too much water, or it will get runny. It is ready when it looks like pancake batter.

2 Set the pizza box on a flat area, and pour the concrete mix into it.

3 Before the concrete mix dries, add the marbles, coins, and other things, pushing them halfway into the concrete mix. Use a stick or pen to write your name, or push your handprint into it (wash your hands immediately).

Now What?

The new stepping stone will dry and seem to harden in two or three days, but leave it alone for at least a week before moving it so it does not crack.

Children's Resource

Children, like grown-ups, learn best by DOING stuff—hands on! But sometimes it is fun to visit someone else's garden to learn more about gardening, or just to see what else you can do to have more fun. Maybe you know a grown-up who has a big garden and loves visitors. Any time you can visit a garden you will learn—and maybe even get some free plants or seeds!

Great Kids' Gardens

There are special places called BOTANICAL GARDENS where you can go to learn more about how things grow. Most have classes for kids, and some even have gardens that are JUST FOR YOU!

Find out about these youth gardens by calling a library or a county extension office, which is part of a university in your state.

Of all the great youth gardens in North America, FOUR really stand out and are worth visiting:

Michigan 4-H Children's Garden

East Lansing, Michigan

Over 60 well-defined theme areas in this award-winning, kid-generated, creative half-acre include a tree house, pond, maze, sundial, and chimes. Brilliant and colorful hands-on specialty gardens feature butterflies, rainbows, storybook tales, education centers, and an outdoor electric train set.

Open from April 1 to October 31; no admission charge.

Prearranged tours are available for a small fee. The garden is located on the Michigan State University campus in East Lansing, about 90 miles northwest of Detroit. For more information call 517-355-0348.

Take a virtual tour of the garden at: www.4hgarden.msu.edu

Everett Children's Adventure Garden

New York Botanical Gardens
Bronx, New York

This garden is an ideal place where kids can let loose their physical energy and imagination and learn about the natural world.

The country's only indoor/outdoor science exploration wonderland covers 12 acres. Children will love more than 40 hands-on nature discovery activities, including mazes, galleries, ponds, trails, indoor and outdoor discovery rooms, oversize botanic and insect specimens, and a nearby 1.5 acre family garden. The garden is at 200th Street & Kazimiroff (Southern) Boulevard, Bronx, New York. Call 718-817-8700 for information. Take a virtual tour at: www.nybg.org/events/stroll.html

Everett Children's Adventure Garden

American Horticultural Society's River Farm

Alexandria, Virginia

Located at George Washington's River Farm on the Potomac River, the Children's Garden includes 10 child scale garden theme areas, including dinosaur, zigzag, vegetable, boat, and alphabet gardens.

River Farm is open to the public Mondays through Fridays, from 8:30 a.m. to 5:00 p.m. It is closed on holidays. Touring the display gardens is free.

The American Horticultural Society is the clearinghouse for youth gardening education programs in the United States. Write to the American Horticultural Society, 7901 East Boulevard Drive in Alexandria, Virginia, or call 703-768-5700 (weekdays). Visit its Website at: www.ahs.org

Heart's Ease

Heart's Ease

Cambria, California

Located along California's central coast, this beautiful garden opened in 1982. The ever-changing Heart's Ease Gardens showcase traditional herb gardens, children's teaching gardens, theme beds, native plant areas, 5-senses garden, a walkway of scented geraniums, and a permanent sunflower house.

The gardens and shop are open daily from 10 a.m. until dusk. The garden is at 4101 Burton Drive in Cambria, California. For information, call 805-927-5224.

American Horticultural Society's River Farm

Finding More Info

Try these web sites

American Horticultural Society: www.ahs.org

National Gardening Association's "Kids and Classrooms": www2.garden.org/nga

Garden Escape "Kids Gardening Camp": www.garden.com

Better Homes and Gardens: www.bhglive/gardening

Backyard Wildlife: www.nwf.org

Libraries and bookstores have books on gardening—some are just for kids who want to learn even more neat stuff to do. You also can use a computer to get great ideas on kids' gardening from the Internet. Some of the best sites have garden experiments you can do for school!

If you are interested in learning about school gardening, any of these places can help you, your parents, or your teachers learn more.

Here are some of the best Internet sites that include kids' gardening information. Ask a grown-up to help you find the Web sites. If you do not want to type in the whole address on the computer, you can do a word search using the group's name. If you do not have a computer, use one at school or at the library.

Great Plants for Kids

How do you know which plants will grow best where you live? Look on the map to find the best ones to start in your region. You can find them easily, as seeds or plants, at a garden center or from a mail-order catalog. They will grow for YOU!

Canada: carrots, beets, bush green beans, corn, nasturtium, zucchini, marigolds, zinnias, sunflowers, snapdragons

Midwest: mint, morning glory, purple coneflower, bulbs (any kind), marigolds, 'Sweet 100' tomatoes, strawberries, "super" petunias, coleus, globe amaranth (Gomphrena)

Ohio Valley: four o'clocks, hyacinth bean, gourds (all kinds), love-in-a-puff (Cardiospermum), carrots (big ones and little ones), spaghetti squash, purple bush beans, sensitive plant (Mimosa), evening primrose, sunflowers

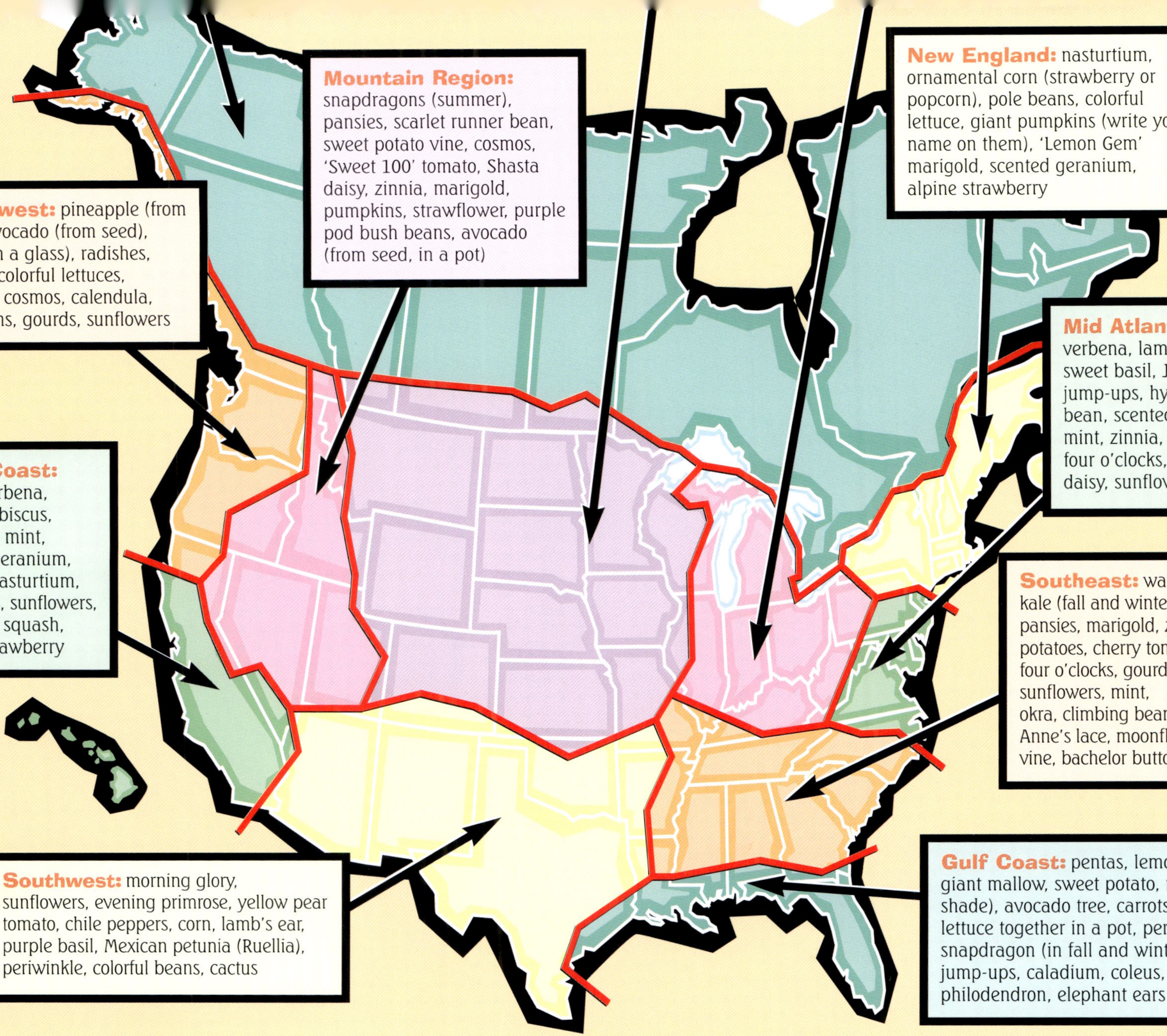

Mountain Region: snapdragons (summer), pansies, scarlet runner bean, sweet potato vine, cosmos, 'Sweet 100' tomato, Shasta daisy, zinnia, marigold, pumpkins, strawflower, purple pod bush beans, avocado (from seed, in a pot)

New England: nasturtium, ornamental corn (strawberry or popcorn), pole beans, colorful lettuce, giant pumpkins (write your name on them), 'Lemon Gem' marigold, scented geranium, alpine strawberry

Northwest: pineapple (from tops), avocado (from seed), bulbs (in a glass), radishes, carrots, colorful lettuces, godetia, cosmos, calendula, pumpkins, gourds, sunflowers

Mid Atlantic: lemon verbena, lamb's ears, sweet basil, Johnny jump-ups, hyacinth bean, scented geranium, mint, zinnia, gourds, four o'clocks, Shasta daisy, sunflowers

West Coast: lemon verbena, zinnia, hibiscus, chocolate mint, scented geranium, gourds, nasturtium, pumpkins, sunflowers, spaghetti squash, alpine strawberry

Southeast: watermelon, kale (fall and winter), pansies, marigold, zinnia, potatoes, cherry tomatoes, four o'clocks, gourds, sunflowers, mint, okra, climbing beans, Queen Anne's lace, moonflower vine, bachelor buttons

Southwest: morning glory, sunflowers, evening primrose, yellow pear tomato, chile peppers, corn, lamb's ear, purple basil, Mexican petunia (Ruellia), periwinkle, colorful beans, cactus

Gulf Coast: pentas, lemon tree, giant mallow, sweet potato, mint (in shade), avocado tree, carrots and lettuce together in a pot, periwinkle, snapdragon (in fall and winter), Johnny jump-ups, caladium, coleus, heart-leaf philodendron, elephant ears

Index

A–F

A-mazing Path, 92-93
Annual, 10
Ants, 12
Anything Bench, 98-99
Aquarium, 32-33
Attracting birds and wildlife, 40-57
Bean Teepee, 70-71
Beans, 60-61
Bees, 7, 40-41
Berries, 12
Bird feeder, 44-45, 50-51
Birdbath, 48-49
Birdhouse, 42-43, 56-57
Birdie Breakfast, 44-45
Birds, 12, 40-45
Boot Kickin' Planter, 16-17
Botanical gardens, 104-106
Bottle Cop Snake, 46-47
Bottle tower, 30-31
Bottles, 16, 20-21, 30-31, 44-45, 76-77, 96-96
Bucket, 8
Buddy Bouquet, 78-79
Bulb, 10
Butterflies, 7, 12, 49, 53
Cactus, 36-37
Candles, 90-91
Canned Music, 88-89
Cans, 16, 26-27, 78-79
Carrots, 66-67
Colors, 76-77
Compost, 10, 24-25, 30-31
Compost Machine, 24-25
Containers, 10, 16-19, 30-39
Corn, 60-61
Cuttings, 23
Decorating the garden, 85-95
Desert Garden, 36-37
Dig, 10
Dinosaurs, 32
Dirt, 6, 10
Dirty Bird's Bath, 48-49
Dryer lint, 50-51
Egg Heads, 38-39
Eggshell, 30-31
Fence, 14-15, 94-95
Fertilizer, 10, 12, 24-25, 31, 41
Finding More Info, 107
Fish, 61
Flavor Garden, 68-69
Flower Shop, 80-81
Flowers, 10, 16-21, 74, 76-81
Flutter-by Garden, 52-53
Food coloring, 20-21, 76-77, 90-91
For the Birds, 50-51
Frogs, 12
Fruit, 10

G–O

Garbage bags, 16
Garden, definition, 14-15
Garden Lantern, 90-91
Garden basics, 4-13
Glass, danger of, 12
Gloves, 9, 86-87
Gourd, 54-57
Grass, 38-39, 92-93
Grass clippings, 25
Grease remover, 18
Great Kids' Gardens, 104-106
Great Plants for Kids, 108-109
Hands, 19
Hat, 12
Herbs, 68-69
Home Tweet Home, 42-43
Hose, 9, 10
How Does Your Gourd Grow? 54-55
Indoor gardening, 28-39

Jurassic Jungle, 32-33
Kitchen scraps, 24-25, 30-31
Knives, safety, 12
Labyrinth, 92-93
Leaves, 6-7, 11, 22, 24
Lettuce, 66-67
Map, 13
Maze, 92-93
Milk jug, 23, 62-63
Mother-in-law plant, 23
Mowing, 92-93
Mulch, 6-7, 11, 64
Multiplying Garden, 22-23
Mushrooms, 12
Nests, birds, 42-43, 50-51
Newspaper strips, 30-31
North America, 13
Notepaper and Pencil, 8
Out of Your Gourd Birdhouse, 56

P–Z

Peanut butter, 50-51
Perennial, 11
Petals, 6-7
Pinecones, 50-51
Pit Stop Planter, 18-19
Plant food, 6, 10, 12
Plant Zones, 13
Planters, 16-21
Poles, 26-27, 54-55, 70-71
Pop Goes the Planter, 20-21
Potatoes, 34-35, 64-65, 81
Potting soil, 8-9, 22, 32, 36
Pots, 8-9, 22, 66-67
Rabbit Chow, 66-67
Raised bed, 20-21
Resources, 102-109
Rocks, 36-37, 48-49
Rootin' Tootin' Potato, 34-35
Roots, 6-7, 11, 22-23, 35
Roy G. Biv Garden, 76-77
Ruler, 9
Safety First, 12
Sand, 23
Scarecrow, 62-63
Scare-dee-crow, 62-63
Scissors, 9, 12
Season, 11, 13
Seeds, 7, 17, 25, 38-39
Shade, 11, 23
Shovel, 8, 21, 25, 96
Shrubs, 7, 11, 23
Snake, 46-47
Soda can, 26-27
Soil, 6-7, 11, 23
Soil & Plant Parts, 6-7
Spiders, 40-41
Sponge, 8, 32-33, 37
Sprouting, 7
Squash, 60-61
Stem, 7, 11, 22
Stepping Stone Jewels, 100-101
String, 8, 15
Sunburn, how to avoid, 12
Sunflower House, 82-83
Sunflower seeds, 61
Sunlight, 6-7, 10-11
Sunscreen, 12
Sweet potatoes, 34-35
Talk Like a Gardener, 10-11
Teeny-Tiny Tomatoes, 72-73
Teepee, 26-27, 54-55, 70-71
Thing Tree, 96-97
Three Sisters Garden, 60-61
Tire planter, 18-19
Toad House, 43
Tomatoes, 72-73
Tools 'n' Stuff, 8-12
Trowel, hand, 9
Trees, 7
Tropical plants, 32-33
Trunks, 7
Tub-O-Taters, 64-65
Turkey baster, 32-33
Vegetables, 11, 60-61, 64-67, 70-73
Vine, 34-35, 54-55, 70-71
Watering can, 9
Wattle Fence, 94-95
Weather Station, 26-27
Web sites, 107
Weed, 11
Wind, 7, 27
Wind chime, 88-89
Wind Glove, 86-87
Wind sock, 87
Worms, 12, 24, 30-31, 32-33
Worm Tower, 30-31
Zones, 13

Metric Conversions

U.S. Units to Metric Equivalent

To Convert From	Multiply By	To Get
Inches	25.4	Millimeters
Inches	2.54	Centimeters
Feet	30.48	Centimeters
Feet	0.3048	Metres
Yards	0.9144	Metres

Metric Units to U.S. Equivalents

To Convert From	Multiply By	To Get
Millimeters	0.0394	Inches
Centimeters	0.3937	Inches
Centimeters	0.0328	Feet
Metres	3.2808	Feet
Metres	1.0936	Yards

Thanks

...to all the people who helped with this book, especially:

The Kids Who Created and Tested All the Projects:

Hayes Berry
Philip Berry
Madeleine Little
Colby Pickett
Ira Rushing
Zoe Rushing

The Regional Garden Experts Who Contributed the Plant Lists:

John Arnold; Albuquerque, New Mexico
Sydney Park Brown; Tampa, Florida
Jeri Cretti; Bennett, Colorado
Anstace Esmonde-White; Kemptville, Ontario, Canada
Ed Hume; Kent, Washington
Sharon Lovejoy; Cambria, California
Ellen Ogden; Londonderry, Vermont
Barbara Pleasant; Lexington, Alabama
Holly Shimizu; Richmond, Virginia
Jane Taylor; Haslett, Michigan
Karen Weir-Jimerson; Des Moines, Iowa

and special thanks to Garden Project/Kid Coordinator: Vickie Hester